LEGENDS OF MAJOR LEAGUE BASEBALL

By Craig Calcaterra

Abbeville Kids
An Imprint of Abbeville Press
New York   London

Statistics are current as of April 25, 2023.
Please note: This book has not been authorized by Major League Baseball.

Project editor: Lauren Orthey
Copy editor: Ashley Benning
Design: Ada Rodriguez
Production director: Louise Kurtz

PHOTOGRAPHY CREDITS

Adobe Stock: cover background (AStakhiv); pp. 2–3 (soupstock); pp. 4–5 (Nattapol_Srtitongcom); pp. 62–63 (Vectorup)

Alamy: cover left (Glasshouse Images); cover center (American Photo Archive); cover right (REUTERS); p. 7 (Everett Collection Inc); p. 9 (RLFE Pix); p. 11 (Francis Specker); p. 15 (Michael Bush); p. 17 (ZUMA Press, Inc.); p. 21 and back cover (ARCHIVIO GBB); p. 23 (RLPM Collection); p. 25 (RLFE Pix); p. 27 (Adam Stoltman); p. 29 (Joe Vella); p. 33 and back cover (Tribune Content Agency LLC); p. 37 (UPI); p. 39 and back cover (RLPM Collection); p. 41 (RLFE Pix); p. 49 (Glasshouse Images); p. 51 (Aflo Co. Ltd.); p. 61 (Glasshouse Images)

Flickr: p. 13 (Bush Foundation); p. 43 (Missouri Historical Society)

Icon Sportswire: p. 55 (Manny Millan)

Library of Congress: p. 19 (National Photo Company); p. 53 (Irwin, La Broad, & Pudlin); p. 59 (Bain News Service)

Wikimedia Commons: p. 31 (Heritage Auctions); p. 35 (Heritage Auctions/New York Yankees); p. 45 (UCLA Library); p. 47 (Sporting News Archive); p. 57 (Bain News Service)

First edition
10 9 8 7 6 5 4 3 2 1

ISBN 978-0-7892-1473-7

Library of Congress Cataloging-in-Publication Data available upon request

For bulk and premium sales and for text adoption procedures, write to Customer Service Manager, Abbeville Press, 655 Third Avenue, New York, NY 10017, or call 1-800-Artbook.

Visit Abbeville Kids online at www.abbeville family.com.

CONTENTS

Henry Aaron

Henry Aaron–known as "Hank"–starred in both football and basketball as a child in Mobile, Alabama, but it was baseball where he truly excelled. Though his family was too poor to afford the equipment, Aaron honed his batting skills by hitting bottle caps with broom handles, helping him develop the quick, powerful wrists that would one day make him among the greatest hitters the game has ever seen.

Aaron's professional career began when he was still a teenager, playing for the Mobile Black Bears and then the Indianapolis Clowns of the Negro Leagues, which were still in existence given Major League Baseball's very slow process of racial integration. In 1952 Aaron's Negro League exploits caused the New York Giants and Boston Braves to take notice and offer him contracts, with Aaron accepting the Braves' higher offer. He'd only play a season and a half in the minor leagues before being called to the majors for the Braves, by then in Milwaukee. Aaron hit his first major league home run on April 23, 1954, and would total 13 in his rookie season. He would not, however, hit fewer than 20 homers in a season for the next 20 years.

Throughout the 1950s, '60s, and early '70s, Aaron was among the best hitters in the game, leading the league in home runs in 1957, 1963, 1966, and 1967, leading the league in RBI in four different seasons, winning two batting titles, and winning the 1957 MVP Award. That year he led the Braves to their first World Series title since 1914–it would be their last World Series title until 1995.

When the Braves moved from Milwaukee to Atlanta after the 1965 season, the hitter-friendly dimensions of the Atlanta–Fulton County Stadium seemed tailor-made for Aaron, allowing him to take his game to a new level at an age when most sluggers began to decline. Throughout the 1960s it was generally thought that if any player might be able to challenge Babe Ruth's all-time home run record, it'd be Mickey Mantle or Willie Mays. Aaron, however, continued to post gaudy home run totals as Mantle and Mays started to slow down, and by the early 1970s, it seemed to be a matter of when, not if, the record would belong to him.

Aaron closed in on Ruth's record in 1973, coming up just short by season's end. Over that off-season he received death threats and hate mail from people who did not want to see a Black man surpass Ruth. While Aaron would later write in his autobiography that the pressure on him was nearly overwhelming, he did not let it affect his performance, and on April 8, 1974, Aaron launched his 715th home run over Atlanta–Fulton County Stadium's left-center field fence and became baseball's Home Run King.

Aaron finished with 755 home runs while setting baseball's all-time RBI record as well. He likewise totaled 3,771 hits, which was second on the all-time list when he retired, and still stands as third. That final number is particularly impressive for a player best known for his home runs. If one were to take away all of Aaron's homers, he'd *still* have more than 3,000 career hits, which is a total that by itself usually earns players admittance to the Hall of Fame.

In light of that, it's fair to say–as many do–that Hank Aaron was the most complete, well-rounded hitter in baseball history.

	AVG	OBP	SLG	OPS+	HR	RBI
6	.305	.374	.555	155	755	2,297

Position: **Outfield**
Batted: **Right**
Threw: **Right**
HT/WT: **6'0", 180 lb.**
Teams: **Milwaukee Braves (1954–65),**
Atlanta Braves (1966–74),
Milwaukee Brewers (1975–76)
Born: **2-5-1934**
Died: **1-22-2021**

Johnny Bench

Perhaps the greatest catcher in the history of the game, Johnny Bench set a new standard for his position during his 17 years in the big leagues, both offensively and defensively. With him both behind and at the plate, his Cincinnati Reds won two World Series titles and four National League pennants and came to be known as "The Big Red Machine."

Bench was drafted by the Reds in the second round of the 1965 amateur draft, but wasn't destined to play in the bush leagues for long. In 1967, he was named the Minor League Player of the Year and made his major league debut that same season. By 1968 Bench was a permanent fixture in the Reds lineup, catching an astounding 154 games and winning that year's Rookie of the Year Award. By 1970 Bench was the National League's Most Valuable Player, putting up a season in which he led the league with 45 homers and drove in 148 runs. He would win his second MVP Award in 1972, smacking 40 homers and driving in 125. He'd lead the league in RBI for a third time in 1974 with 129.

It was Bench's defense, however, which was truly exceptional. He was renowned as having the strongest throwing arm in the game, which was particularly important in the 1960s and '70s, when base stealing was far more common. He also had huge hands—he could famously hold seven baseballs in one hand at once—which aided him in retrieving the ball from his glove quickly and firing down to second base. He was innovative as well, being one of the first catchers to catch with one arm behind his back to protect it from foul tips. He was also an early adopter of a hinged catcher's mitt, rather than the then-popular circular "pillow"-style mitts, which allowed him to make plays on bunts more easily. Bench won Gold Gloves in his first 10 seasons, and they were well-earned. He now, arguably, stands as the greatest defensive catcher in baseball history.

Beyond his offensive and defensive exploits, Bench was a respected team leader and, at times, served as an unofficial coach or manager for the Reds. Even when he was in his early 20s, he gave pointers to his pitchers, devised game plans for opposing hitters, and would tell his manager Sparky Anderson if a pitcher should be taken out of a game or allowed to stay in. While such assertiveness from a young player often annoys teammates, Bench's came to respect his judgment and leadership without question.

Bench continued to play until 1983, spending his final years at third base and, occasionally, first base due to the wear and tear of catching on his knees. He'd finish with nearly 400 career home runs and earned himself a first-ballot election to the Hall of Fame in 1989 with over 96 percent of the vote.

AVG	OBP	SLG	OPS+	HR	RBI
.267	.342	.476	126	389	1,376

Position: **Catcher**
Batted: **Right**
Threw: **Right**
HT/WT: **6'1", 197 lb.**
Team: **Cincinnati Reds (1967–83)**
Born: **12-7-1947**

Barry Bonds

It's always difficult to compare players from different eras, so whether one thinks that Babe Ruth, Hank Aaron, or Barry Bonds is the greatest home run hitter of all time is open for debate. It is not hyperbole, however, to say that Bonds would be one of the three or four finalists in a contest to name the greatest hitter who ever lived. And there's a very strong argument to be made that he is the most *feared* hitter to ever live.

Barry's father, Bobby Bonds, was a 14-year major league veteran who made three All-Star teams himself and in his day possessed one of the best combinations of power and speed. Fellow legend Willie Mays was a teammate of Bobby and is Barry's godfather. Young Barry Bonds had unsurpassed mentors, all but ensuring that he would play the game. After starring in football, basketball, and baseball in high school, Bonds accepted a scholarship to baseball powerhouse Arizona State University where he emerged as one of the top amateur players in the country. He was selected by the Pittsburgh Pirates in the first round of the 1985 draft and made his major league debut early in the 1986 season.

Bonds's on-the-field accomplishments in his 22-year big league career are legion. In 2001 he set the record for most home runs in a season with 73, and in 2007 he passed Hank Aaron to become the all-time home run leader, finishing his career with 762 round trippers. But there was much, much more to Bonds's game than mere home runs.

Bonds makes the list of many all-time records: second place in extra-base hits and total times on base, fourth in OPS and third in OPS+ (which adjusts for the era and ballparks played in), third in runs scored, sixth in on-base percentage, sixth in slugging percentage, and sixth in RBI. Bonds also holds the record for most MVP Awards with seven and probably deserved to win it a couple more times based on his accomplishments. Bonds holds the all-time record for putouts by a left fielder; he won eight Gold Glove Awards and stole 514 bases in his career, making him a more accomplished power-speed player than his father and, in the minds of many, his godfather Mays. Indeed, there was not a facet of the game in which he did not excel.

As for being the most feared hitter of all time, simply look at how little opposing teams pitched to him. Bonds is both the all-time leader in walks and holds the top-three single season marks for walks. He is likewise the all-time leader in *intentional* walks, which is when the opposing team walks a hitter on purpose rather than attempting to pitch to him. As a testament to how feared a hitter Bonds was, in 1998 the Arizona Diamondbacks walked Bonds with the bases loaded, choosing to give the Giants a free run rather than let him swing the bat.

Despite Bonds's prodigious accomplishments, he has not been elected to the Baseball Hall of Fame due to using performance-enhancing drugs to improve his game. That dealt Bonds a severe reputational blow and has caused many to question the validity of his record. But the fact that he was one of the greatest players in the game's history and, without question, the greatest hitter of his era cannot be disputed.

AVG	OBP	SLG	OPS+	HR	RBI
.298	.444	.607	182	762	1,996

Position: **Outfield**
Batted: **Left**
Threw: **Left**
HT/WT: **6'1", 185 lb.**
Teams: **Pittsburgh Pirates (1986–92), San Francisco Giants (1993–2007)**
Born: **7-24-1964**

Oscar Charleston

Oscar Charleston, who spent 43 years in baseball as a player, manager, and scout, is considered by many to have been the greatest player in the history of the Negro Leagues. Though only around 5'8", Charleston was a phenomenal all-around athlete, possessed of great speed, great power, a keen batting eye, a fantastic glove, and superior baseball instincts and intellect. There was simply no aspect of the game in which he did not excel, and though the stories of Negro League players of his era are sometimes embellished, there is little dispute regarding Charleston's greatness.

A native of Indianapolis, Indiana, Charleston first played baseball on sandlots and then in the army. He began playing professionally with the Indianapolis ABCs at the age of 20 but, as was common among Black players of his era, was constantly on the move, joining new teams for better offers or because his clubs were experiencing financial difficulties. He also spent a great deal of time barnstorming from town to town, playing for numerous teams in both the official Negro Leagues and in various independent leagues, a regular practice in the early 20th century. Throughout his career he was player-manager for several teams as well, and when he was done playing, he continued to manage until his death. He also spent time as an umpire, and following the desegregation of the American and National Leagues, he served as a scout for the Brooklyn Dodgers. It was on Charleston's recommendation, in fact, that the club signed Hall of Fame catcher Roy Campanella, among others.

While statistics for Negro League players were hard to come by for many years and were often unreliable, Charleston's prodigious accomplishments are nevertheless clear. In many years early in his career he hit over .400, garnering comparisons to Ty Cobb, and Major League Baseball officially lists him as a career .365 hitter, which is among the highest career marks of all time. He led the Negro Leagues in batting, home runs, hits, stolen bases, and RBI in multiple seasons during the 1920s, and his defensive exploits were frequently mentioned in news accounts of the day.

Word of mouth may be the most reliable barometer of Charleston's prowess, however, with fellow baseball legend Honus Wagner declaring Charleston as the best player he had ever seen and Hall of Fame manager John McGraw once saying, "If Oscar Charleston isn't the greatest baseball player in the world, then I'm no judge of baseball talent." In more recent years any number of scouts, analysts, and writers have placed him among legends such as Babe Ruth, Willie Mays, and Wagner himself as one of the greatest players of all time.

Positions: **Outfield, First Base**
Batted: **Left**
Threw: **Left**
HT/WT: **5'8", 185 lb.**
Teams: **Indianapolis ABCs (1920), St. Louis Giants (1921), Indianapolis ABCs (1922–23), Harrisburg Giants (1924–27), Hilldale Daisies (1929), Homestead Grays (1929), Pittsburgh Crawfords (1933–38), Philadelphia Stars (1941)**
Born: **10-14-1896**
Died: **10-5-1954**

AVG	OBP	SLG	OPS+	HR	RBI
.365	.449	.615	184	143	853

Roger Clemens

There are few pitchers who have accomplished what Roger "Rocket" Clemens did in his 24-year major league career. He won a record seven Cy Young Awards, posted 354 victories, struck out 4,672 batters, was a seven-time ERA leader, a six-time 20-game winner, and a five-time strikeout leader. He tossed 46 shutouts and was the ace of two World Series champions. There was never a time when Clemens was not considered one of the best, if not the very best, pitchers in the game.

Clemens's story, however, is not one of complete triumph. While a nearly supernatural level of ambition–matched by a nearly supernatural work ethic–allowed him to ascend to the top of the game, it ultimately caused him to do things that cast him in a negative light and prevented him from being inducted into the Hall of Fame.

Born in Ohio but raised in Texas, Clemens was a late bloomer compared to many star pitchers, failing to stand out as a high schooler or gain much notice from colleges or big league programs. Under the tutelage of legendary college coach Wayne Graham, though, Clemens took his game to the next level in his sole season at Houston's San Jacinto Junior College and transferred to the University of Texas where he led the Longhorns to a College World Series victory in 1983. That year he was selected in the first round of the draft by the Boston Red Sox. Then, following less than a full year in the minors, he made his major league debut in 1984.

Clemens's first two years in the big leagues were a learning process for him, in which he occasionally flashed brilliance but often showed his temper and aggression while gaining a reputation for throwing at batters' heads. In 1986, however, he got it all together, winning his first 14 decisions, and on April 28 of that year he set a major league record by striking out 20 batters in a victory over the Seattle Mariners. Clemens would win both the Cy Young and MVP Awards that season while leading the Red Sox to an American League title and a seven-game loss in the World Series.

From then on Clemens was never anything but a superstar, collecting a second Cy Young Award in 1987, a third in 1991, a fourth and fifth in 1997 and 1998 after signing with the Toronto Blue Jays, and two more while pitching for the Yankees in 2001 and the Astros in 2004. Clemens's longevity in the game was notable. He'd retire following the 2003 season only to unretire and did so again before the 2006 and 2007 seasons as well–each time lured back to the game he loved. His final appearance came in a playoff loss for the Yankees in October 2007.

Soon after the 2007 season Clemens was named repeatedly in the Mitchell Report, which exposed the use of performance-enhancing drugs among major league players. Clemens's ambition, it seems, kept him from being content with mere greatness.

Position: **Starting Pitcher**
Batted: **Right**
Threw: **Right**
HT/WT: **6'4", 205 lb.**
Teams: **Boston Red Sox (1984–96), Toronto Blue Jays (1997–98), New York Yankees (1999–2003, 2007), Houston Astros (2004–6)**
Born: **8-4-1962**

W	L	ERA	ERA+	IP	K	BB
354	184	3.12	143	4,916.2	4,672	1,580

Roberto Clemente

Every player in this book was a superstar. Only Roberto Clemente, however, was both a superstar and a true hero. He was so much of a hero that his baseball accomplishments, while outstanding, take a back seat to his personal courage and sacrifice.

Clemente was born in 1934 in Carolina, Puerto Rico, where he excelled at track and field and baseball in his teens, with many citing his proficiency at javelin aiding what would eventually be considered one of baseball's best all-time throwing arms. Following his stardom in youth baseball in Puerto Rico, the Brooklyn Dodgers–wowed by Clemente's quick bat, fleet feet, and absolute cannon of a right arm–put him under contract in 1952, signing him to a hefty bonus. Following the 1954 season, however, the Dodgers left Clemente off the team's major league roster which, under the rules at the time for players who received large bonuses, allowed him to be selected by another team in an off-season draft. This would turn out to be one of the Dodgers' greatest mistakes, but for the Pittsburgh Pirates, who drafted Clemente, it was one of the greatest steals in baseball history.

Clemente's first five seasons in the majors were often a struggle, as he worked to remain a consistent hitter and adjust to life in the majors both on and off the field, as someone whose first language was Spanish. He came into his own in 1960, hitting .312, making the All-Star team, and helping lead the Pirates to the World Series title, upsetting the mighty New York Yankees.

During the next seven years, Clemente won four National League batting titles and the 1966 NL Most Valuable Player Award and began a string of 12 straight Gold Glove Award seasons in right field. In 1967, Clemente hit a career-high .357, scored 23 home runs, and knocked in 110 runs. Following that season a group of major league general managers were polled and declared Clemente "the best player in baseball today."

In 1971, the 37-year-old Clemente led Pittsburgh back to the World Series, where he helped the Pirates win another championship and was named the World Series MVP. Clemente recorded his 3,000th career hit late in the 1972 season, becoming just the 11th player to reach the milestone to that point. No one then knew that hit number 3,000 would be the last of Roberto Clemente's career.

In late December 1972 a massive earthquake struck Nicaragua. Clemente, who had engaged in considerable charitable work over the course of his career, helped organize airlifts of needed supplies from Puerto Rico to Nicaragua. Following reports that these supplies had been diverted by corrupt government officials, Clemente decided to accompany the next load himself. To that end, on December 31, 1972, Clemente boarded a small plane bound for Managua. Sadly, the heavily loaded plane developed engine trouble and crashed off the Puerto Rican coast soon after takeoff, killing Clemente and the others on board.

Clemente, long a hero on the field, died a hero off of it. In his honor, Major League Baseball waived the traditional five-year waiting period for players to be eligible for the Hall of Fame and Clemente was elected in 1973.

AVG	OBP	SLG	OPS+	HR	RBI
.317	.359	.475	130	240	1,305

Position: **Outfield**
Batted: **Right**
Threw: **Right**
HT/WT: **5'11", 175 lb.**
Team: **Pittsburgh Pirates
(1955–72)**
Born: **8-18-1934**
Died: **12-31-1972**

Ty Cobb

Ty Cobb, nicknamed "The Georgia Peach" after his home state, has the highest career major league batting average of all time, won a record 12 American League batting championships, and led the league in OPS+ nine times in a row and 10 times overall. He likewise finished his career as the all-time stolen base leader and stands at fourth on the all-time list. While some are partial to Ruth and Mays, Cobb remains among the small handful of players with a claim to the title of greatest player in baseball history.

Born into a prominent family in a small farming community in Georgia known as The Narrows, Cobb was expected to get an education and find his way into business, politics, medicine, or law. Cobb wanted none of that, and instead attended a tryout organized by a minor league team in Augusta, Georgia, eventually joining the club. In 1905 the Detroit Tigers trained in Augusta, were impressed by Cobb, and signed him. That same month, however, his mother shot and killed his father. The Ty Cobb that arrived in Detroit that summer was a changed young man, serious and angry. While Cobb's immense hitting talents would define his career, his reaction to the tragedy of his father's death would define him for the rest of his life.

Following a rough first two years in Detroit, Cobb emerged as a superstar in 1907, winning the first of three consecutive batting titles—and the first three of 10 overall for Detroit—by hitting .350 and leading the Tigers to their first pennant. Another batting title and pennant followed in 1908, and in 1909, Cobb won the AL Triple Crown, leading the league in batting average, home runs, and runs batted in, and helping the Tigers to their third straight World Series. At the same time, his reputa-tion for irritability and pugnaciousness grew, with Cobb getting into fistfights with opposing players, fans, and, on one occasion, a hotel security guard which led to Cobb's arrest and an eventual guilty plea to a charge of assault and battery.

From the time he won the Triple Crown until the emergence of Babe Ruth as a power hitter in 1919, Cobb was universally acknowledged not only as the best player in baseball, but as arguably the greatest of all time. He would win the batting title year after year and place among the league leaders in all important hitting categories. Controversy continued to follow him as well, with Cobb getting embroiled in feuds with other players, the league office, and his own team's owner. None of this slowed him down on the field, as he hit over .400 three times, in 1911, 1912, and 1922.

Cobb became the Tigers player-manager in 1921 and would finish his career with the Philadelphia Athletics. He had played for 24 years in the majors, and the only time he batted under .300 came in his short, 41-game rookie campaign. He was elected to the Hall of Fame's inaugural class in 1936, receiving the most votes of the five original inductees.

Position: **Outfield**
Batted: **Left**
Threw: **Right**
HT/WT: **6'1", 175 lb.**
Teams: **Detroit Tigers (1905–26), Philadelphia Athletics (1927–28)**
Born: **12-18-1886**
Died: **7-17-1961**

AVG	OBP	SLG	OPS+	HR	RBI
.366	.433	.512	168	117	1,944

Lou Gehrig

Wally Pipp was the starting first baseman for the New York Yankees from 1915 to 1924. On June 2, 1925, Pipp woke up with a headache and asked his manager Miller Huggins for the day off. The man who replaced Pipp at first base that day was Lou Gehrig. Gehrig would go on to play every single game for the Yankees from that day until his retirement in 1939. Pipp, who had made way for one of the best players in the game's history, would later say, "I took the two most expensive aspirins in history."

Gehrig, a soft-spoken and polite man, was a native of New York City who first came to prominence as a player for Columbia University. While he is known for playing in a then-record 2,130 consecutive games, which earned him the nickname "The Iron Horse," he was far more than just a consistent presence in the Yankees lineup. Indeed, he was one of the game's greatest hitters, combining outstanding batting average (.340), power (493 home runs and 1,995 RBI), plate patience (1,508 walks), and speed (163 triples). Gehrig scored more than 100 runs and recorded at least 100 RBI for 13 straight seasons in his 14 as an everyday player. He led the American League in runs four times, home runs three times, RBI five times, on-base percentage five times, and batting average once. He finished among the league's top-three hitters in batting average seven times and had eight 200-plus-hit seasons. In 1931, he set the American League record with 185 RBI. He won the Triple Crown in 1934, hitting .363, smacking 49 home runs, and driving in 166 runs.

Though in his first several seasons Gehrig was overshadowed by his more famous teammate Babe Ruth, he was by no means a second banana. The Yankees saw just as much—if not more—success after Ruth's departure in 1936, when the team was led by Gehrig, with four of their seven American League pennants won after the Babe left. Gehrig's own World Series production consisted of a .361 batting average, 10 home runs, and 35 RBI in 34 games.

In late 1938 Gehrig began to suffer from muscle pain, dizziness, and coordination problems, and early in the 1939 season he asked to be taken out of the lineup. He received a grim diagnosis: amyotrophic lateral sclerosis, or ALS, which is a disease that causes fatal and incurable paralysis. The disease would soon come to be commonly known as Lou Gehrig's disease. He would never play another game.

On July 4, 1939, the Yankees held "Lou Gehrig Day" on which Gehrig's former teammates, government officials, and other VIPs showed up to pay tribute to the stricken hero. That afternoon Gehrig gave a speech to a sold-out Yankee Stadium which would go down in history as one of the finest, most inspiring moments of American oratory, with Gehrig saying the immortal words, "For the past two weeks you have been reading about a bad break. Today I consider myself the luckiest man on the face of the earth."

Gehrig was elected to the Hall of Fame that same year. His accomplishments and his courage will never be forgotten.

Position: **First Base**
Batted: **Left**
Threw: **Left**
HT/WT: **6', 200 lb.**
Team: **New York Yankees (1923–39)**
Born: **6-19-1903**
Died: **6-2-1941**

AVG	OBP	SLG	OPS+	HR	RBI
.340	.447	.632	179	493	1,995

Josh Gibson

Josh Gibson is considered by many to be the greatest power hitter of all time, with skills equaling or even surpassing those of Ruth and Aaron. And though his career and life were short, his legend was large and remains enduring.

Gibson was born in Buena Vista, Georgia, but his family moved to Pittsburgh in 1923 when his father took a job in a steel mill. Gibson dropped out of school in the ninth grade and began playing for a local semipro team. He caught his big break while sitting in the stands at a Homestead Grays game when Grays catcher Buck Ewing was injured. By this time Gibson's reputation for long home runs was well-known around Pittsburgh, and he was asked to fill in for Ewing on a temporary basis. Though Gibson was still too young to stick with the Grays for the long term, the stint launched his professional career.

Following a season with another semipro club in Memphis and various barnstorming stints in the Mexican, Puerto Rican, and Cuban leagues, Gibson would spend the remainder of his career playing for Pittsburgh's two powerhouse clubs, the Crawfords and the Grays, while making off-season sojourns to play in Latin America. Such a patchwork career, and the patchwork manner in which statistics were kept in those days, can make tallying Negro League players' accomplishments difficult, but it is generally accepted that Gibson hit nearly 800 home runs in league games, independent games, and barnstorming games combined over the course of his career, even if he hit "only" 166 in official Negro

League contests. It should be noted, of course, that Negro League seasons were considerably shorter than American League and National League seasons and that Gibson's home run rate–estimated to be one home run for roughly every 15 at bats–is comparable to those of the top home run hitters of all time.

Whatever one thinks of the statistical record, the anecdotal accounts of Gibson's accomplishments make it clear that his power was unsurpassed.

Sporting News, which was baseball's primary written authority for decades, credits Gibson with hitting a 580-foot home run in Yankee Stadium. There is no photographic or contemporaneous evidence of that feat, but if verified, it would qualify as the longest home run ever hit. Less speculatively, Washington Senators owner Clark Griffith once said that Gibson hit more home runs into Griffith Stadium's distant left field bleachers than any player in the American League ever did. Nearly every interview of Negro League players who played with or against Gibson contains similar stories about the frequency and distance of Gibson's home runs.

Sadly, Gibson died of a stroke at 35, just three months before Jackie Robinson became the first Black player in the then-established major leagues. Had he been born later or, more to the point, if the major leagues had ended their policy of segregation earlier, Gibson would have been appreciated by more baseball fans, and his fame and renown would have been larger in his own lifetime.

AVG	OBP	SLG	OPS+	HR	RBI
.373	.458	.718	214	166	733

Position: **Catcher**
Batted: **Right**
Threw: **Right**
HT/WT: **6'1", 220 lb.**
Teams: **Memphis Red Sox (1930),
Pittsburgh Crawfords (1933–36),
Homestead Grays (1937–40, 1942–46)**
Born: **12-21-1911**
Died: **1-20-1947**

Lefty Grove

Robert Moses "Lefty" Grove is generally considered to be the greatest left-handed pitcher of all time, with Warren Spahn, Sandy Koufax, and Randy Johnson the only others with possible claims to that title. Grove, however, was more consistent and more dominant than his fellow Hall of Fame southpaws, having won over two-thirds of his lifetime decisions and having posted the second-highest career ERA+ in history, trailing fellow legend Pedro Martínez.

Grove was born into a coal-mining family in Lonaconing, Maryland, and rather than play baseball in organized youth leagues, he learned to pitch by throwing rocks. After winning a tryout with a low-level minor league team in Martinsburg, Virginia, he was discovered by the owner of the then-minor league Baltimore Orioles, Jack Dunn, the same man who had discovered Ruth a few years before.

Back in those days the minor leagues were not as closely affiliated to major league teams as they are today, and the idea of young stars being "called up" to the big leagues the moment their skills were honed was not established. So Grove remained with the Orioles for five seasons—until he was 25 years old—before Dunn finally sold Grove's contract to the major league Philadelphia Athletics. By that time Grove had won 108 International League decisions and was quite a major star and box office draw in Baltimore. As a result, he commanded a price of $100,600, an astronomical sum for the time.

Having emerged as a fully seasoned pro, Grove accomplished the rare feat of leading the league in strikeouts as a rookie in 1925. He would continue to lead the league in strikeouts for the next five years after that as well, while picking up the American League ERA title in 1926. The Athletics teams managed to surpass the Babe Ruth/Lou Gehrig Yankees for the AL pennant in 1929, 1930, and 1931–winning the World Series in the first two years of that run–in large part due to Grove's formidable presence on the mound. Grove won 20 games against only six losses in 1929, once again leading the league in ERA. He was even better the next two years, going 28–5 in 1930 and 31–4 in 1931, leading the league in wins, ERA, and strikeouts in each of those years, thereby earning the pitching Triple Crown.

Following the 1933 season Athletics owner Connie Mack traded away many of his stars in order to cut payroll, and Grove was sent to the Red Sox. Though an arm injury limited his effectiveness in his first season in Boston, Grove returned to form in 1935, winning 20 games and once again leading the league in ERA with a mark of 2.70. He'd win his seventh ERA title in 1936, his eighth in 1938, and a ninth in 1939. No other pitcher in major league history has won as many ERA titles, with the next-closest competitor being Clemens with seven. Grove remained an above-average pitcher in 1940 and, in 1941, at 41, he won his 300th and final major league game.

Grove was elected to the Hall of Fame in 1947.

W	L	ERA	ERA+	IP	K	BB
300	141	3.06	148	3,940.2	2,266	1,187

Position: **Starting Pitcher**
Batted: **Left**
Threw: **Left**
HT/WT: **6'3", 190 lb.**
Teams: **Philadelphia Athletics (1925–33), Boston Red Sox (1934–41)**
Born: **3-6-1900**
Died: **5-22-1975**

Rickey Henderson

There might not have been any player in history who was better at more things than Rickey Henderson. He was, without question, the greatest leadoff hitter and the greatest base stealer of all time. He arguably possessed the greatest combination of power and speed of any player in the history of the game as well. Perhaps the best characterization of Henderson's career came from baseball historian and analyst Bill James: "If you could split Rickey Henderson in two, you'd have *two* Hall of Famers."

Born on Christmas Day in 1958 in Chicago, Henderson spent most of his childhood in Oakland, California. Despite being offered multiple football scholarships as a running back, Henderson chose the national pastime instead after being drafted by his hometown Athletics.

In 1980, his first full major league season, Henderson broke Ty Cobb's 65-year-old American League record for stolen bases by swiping 100 bags to Cobb's 96. In 1982 he stole 130 bases, breaking Hall of Famer Lou Brock's all-time single-season record of 118. Henderson's 130 steals that year stand as the record to this day. He would lead the American League in stolen bases in each of his first seven full seasons and nine of his first 10. He'd lead his league in steals in 12 seasons in all, the last of which came when he was 39 years old. On May 1, 1991, he broke Brock's all-time stolen base record with his 939th steal and would go on to steal an astounding 1,406 bases before he retired. No player has come anywhere close in the three decades since, and many doubt anyone ever will top Henderson.

Henderson's ability to get on base set him apart from other speedsters. Part of that was because he was a great hitter, having finished in the top 10 in batting average on multiple occasions. It was also because of his extraordinary batting eye. Henderson led the league in walks four times, finishing in the top 10 on 17 occasions, and placed in the top 10 in on-base percentage in 16 different seasons. As a result of being on base so often—and thanks to tremendous conditioning which allowed him to play for 25 seasons—Henderson is the all-time leader in runs scored, passing Cobb's mark in 2001.

Henderson's power was considerable as well, as evidenced by his nearly 300 career homers, which is a tremendous number for a leadoff hitter. Eighty-one of those home runs led off games, which is yet another record he holds. His status as a great all-around player is also evidenced by his 10 All-Star selections, winning the 1990 MVP Award, and by every one of the many teams he joined during his career seeming to immediately improve once he arrived.

Henderson's career cannot be boiled down to mere statistics, however. He was a larger-than-life star known for his colorful quotes, flamboyant personality, and no small amount of self-promotion. While some critics took issue with what they perceived to be Henderson's ego, the player backed it all up with a phenomenal work ethic, evidenced by one of his most famous quotes: "If my uniform doesn't get dirty, I haven't done anything in the baseball game."

Rickey Henderson's uniform was almost always dirty because Rickey did it all.

AVG	OBP	SLG	OPS+	HR	RBI
.279	.401	.419	127	297	1,115

Position: **Outfield**
Batted: **Right**
Threw: **Left**
HT/WT: **5'10", 180 lb.**
Teams: **Oakland Athletics (1979–84, 1989–93, 1994–95, 1998), New York Yankees (1985–89), Toronto Blue Jays (1993), San Diego Padres (1996–97), California Angels (1997), New York Mets (1999–2000), Seattle Mariners (2000), San Diego Padres (2001), Boston Red Sox (2002), Los Angeles Dodgers (2003)**
Born: **12-25-1958**

Rogers Hornsby

Rogers Hornsby was such a good hitter that it was said that even the umpires trusted his judgment more than their own. One story told about him—which was likely legend rather than fact—spoke of a time a pitcher complained that an umpire called a close pitch to Hornsby a ball rather than strike three. The umpire told the pitcher, "Son, Mr. Hornsby will tell you when it's close enough to be a strike."

Of course, one need not tell tall tales about Hornsby in order to explain his greatness, because the facts speak for themselves.

Hornsby, born and raised in Texas, took a job at a meatpacking plant when he was just 10 years old and was asked to join its industrial league team soon after, despite being several years younger than the next-oldest player. He was then recruited to a semiprofessional team when he was just 15. From there he was asked to join a low-level minor league team in Texas where he caught the attention of scouts from the St. Louis Cardinals, who signed him when he was still only 19. He'd make his major league debut soon after.

It only took about a year for the young Hornsby to adjust to major league pitching, and by his third year he led the National League in triples, slugging, OPS, and OPS+. In 1920 he was moved from shortstop, where he often struggled defensively, to second base. That move coincided with Hornsby exploding offensively and leading the NL in the three most important rate stats: batting average, on-base percentage, and slugging percentage. He repeated the feat in every season between 1920 and 1925 and again in 1928.

Hornsby's best season, 1922, may have been the single most dominant season by any player in the history of baseball. That year he not only won the Triple Crown, leading the league in average, home runs, and runs batted in, but came out on top in seven major offensive categories in all. And he didn't just lead—he dominated, posting an average 50 points higher than the second-place finisher, hitting 16 more home runs than anyone else, leading the league in RBI by 20, in hits by 35, in total bases by 136, and slugging 150 percentage points higher than anyone.

In all he won seven National League batting titles and hit over .400 three times, including a mark of .424 in 1924, the second-highest mark of all time. Hornsby's .358 lifetime batting average is second only to Ty Cobb's. And, though the record has since been surpassed many times, when he retired Hornsby stood as the all-time home run leader among National Leaguers.

But even if Rogers Hornsby could be hard to play for, no one questioned his love for the game. When asked how he spent his off-seasons, he replied: "People ask me what I do in winter when there's no baseball. I'll tell you what I do. I stare out the window and wait for spring."

Position: **Second Base**
Batted: **Right**
Threw: **Right**
HT/WT: **5'11", 175 lb.**
Teams: **St. Louis Cardinals (1915–26), New York Giants (1927), Boston Braves (1928), Chicago Cubs (1929–32), St. Louis Cardinals (1933), St. Louis Browns (1933–37)**
Born: **4-27-1896**
Died: **1-5-1963**

AVG	OBP	SLG	OPS+	HR	RBI
.358	.434	.577	175	301	1,584

Walter Johnson

Walter Johnson came late to baseball, not playing in any organized leagues until his midteens. Later in life Johnson credited that for his almost completely injury-free career, believing that by waiting until his body matured he did not put unnecessary strain on growing muscles. Whether that was the reason for his remarkable stamina and health is hard to say, but it is true that Johnson's unusual, self-taught pitching delivery, characterized by an easy, sidearm motion, allowed him to deliver his pitches with an economy of effort that nonetheless generated tremendous velocity. While radar guns had not yet been invented and so the actual speed of his pitches can't be known, Johnson's speed earned him the nickname "The Big Train," and for 21 big league seasons he was the most dominant pitcher in baseball. After playing only two years of amateur ball, Johnson signed on with a low-level minor league team in Idaho. Word of his outstanding fastball reached Washington Senators manager Joe Cantillon, who signed Johnson immediately.

Johnson only pitched in part of his rookie 1907 season due to signing late in the year and got another late start in 1908 after a serious ear infection. On Labor Day weekend of that year, however, Johnson announced his presence with authority. The 20-year-old Johnson started three consecutive games against the New York Highlanders, shutting them out in all three while allowing only six, four, and two hits, respectively. No modern pitcher would dare start three consecutive games, and even if they did, it'd be unthink-able that they'd shut down the opposition. It was truly one of the most remarkable performances of his or any other generation, but Johnson was only getting started.

Despite playing for a poor Washington team with few offensive superstars, Johnson won no fewer than 25 games between 1910 and 1916–winning an amazing 36 games in 1913–and leading the American League in wins all four years from 1913 through 1916. He'd lead the league in wins again in 1918 and 1924 and would finish with 417 in his career, which is second for all time behind Cy Young.

Strikeouts, however, are what Johnson is best known for. He led the league in strikeouts a record 12 times and punched out a phenomenal 3,509 batters, which was a record he held for 56 years. From the end of his career in 1927 until 1974, Johnson was the only pitcher to strike out as many as 3,000 batters, and he remains the only pitcher in history to record over 400 wins and strike out over 3,500 batters.

Johnson after having poor teams for nearly two decades, finally made the World Series in 1924 with the Senators. Despite already having started twice in the Series, the 36-year-old Johnson shut out the New York Giants for four innings to earn the victory and give the Senators their only World Series championship.

Johnson retired after the 1927 season having accomplished everything a player could. He remains, to this day, one of the greatest pitchers in the history of the game.

W	L	ERA	ERA+	IP	K	BB
417	279	2.17	147	5,914.1	3,509	1,363

Position: **Starting Pitcher**
Batted: **Right**
Threw: **Right**
HT/WT: **6'1", 200 lb.**
Team: **Washington Senators (1907–27)**
Born: **11-6-1887**
Died: **12-10-1946**

Greg Maddux

Greg Maddux was the most dominant National League pitcher of his era, posting minuscule ERAs at a time when sluggers otherwise were ascendant and offense, not pitching, ruled the game. He did so by demonstrating astounding control, walking fewer batters than any of his peers and putting the baseball seemingly wherever he wanted it to go.

Maddux was born in Texas but moved around frequently as a child due to his father's service in the U.S. Air Force. He learned the game from his older brother Mike, who would become a major league pitcher and, later, a respected pitching coach. Maddux attended Valley High School in Las Vegas, Nevada, his father's final station, and it was there his talents truly blossomed. He led his team to the Nevada state championship in 1983. In 1984 he was drafted in the second round by the Chicago Cubs, making his major league debut in 1986.

After two seasons of growing pains Maddux came into his own in 1988, posting a record of 18–8 and beginning a run of 17 straight seasons with at least 15 victories, which is the longest streak in big league history. Maddux also earned the first of his eight All-Star Game selections that year. In 1989, Maddux went 19–12 with a 2.95 ERA, leading the Cubs to the NL East title. In 1990 Maddux won the first of 18 Gold Glove Awards, the most by any player at any position in baseball history.

And then he got even better. In 1992, Maddux won 20 games while posting a league-best 2.18 ERA. That earned him the first of four straight Cy Young Awards, which remains tied for the most consecutive Cy Youngs in history. After the season Maddux signed with the Atlanta Braves on a five-year, $28 million deal—one of the biggest bargains in major league history.

Maddux won 20 games and posted a league-best 2.36 ERA in 1993. In 1994 and 1995 he posted ERAs of 1.56 and 1.63, respectively, which were the second and third-lowest ERAs since 1968. Given the far more hitter-friendly offensive environment of the mid-1990s, however, Maddux's ERAs were even more impressive as reflected by his higher ERA+ figures of 271 and 260. Maddox would lead the Braves to a World Series title in 1995; his team went to three World Series in all, and they won their division in each of the 11 completed seasons in which he played in Atlanta.

Perhaps even more impressive than Maddux's win and ERA totals was his phenomenal control. In 889.1 innings pitched in 1994–97, Maddux walked only 102 batters, 23 of which were intentional free passes. It's simply unheard of for a pitcher to issue so few walks today.

Maddux returned to the Cubs in 2004, then had stints with the Los Angeles Dodgers and San Diego Padres. Even in his declining years, he remained an above-average pitcher, allowing him to pitch into his 23rd season before retiring in 2008. He finished with 355 wins and only 227 losses, which amounted to a fantastic .610 winning percentage. His victory total is the eighth best of all time, and his innings pitched total of 5,008.1 ranks 13th. Maddux was elected to the Hall of Fame in 2014.

W	L	ERA	ERA+	IP	K	BB
355	227	3.16	132	5,008.1	3,371	999

Position: **Starting Pitcher**

Batted: **Right**

Threw: **Right**

HT/WT: **6', 170 lb.**

Teams: **Chicago Cubs (1986–92, 2004–6), Atlanta Braves, (1993–2003), Los Angeles Dodgers (2006, 2008), San Diego Padres (2007, 2008)**

Born: **4-14-1966**

Mickey Mantle

The Yankees teams dominating baseball from the 1920s through the 1960s were loaded with Hall of Famers and superstars. The dynasty can be roughly broken up into three different phases: The 1920s into the 1930s were the Babe Ruth/Lou Gehrig years. In the late 1930s until 1950 Joe DiMaggio was the top player. Mantle played for the Bronx Bombers from 1951 to his retirement after the 1968 season, and in those years, there was not a bigger star in all of baseball.

Mantle's father Elvin, a lead and zinc miner from Commerce, Oklahoma, and his grandfather Charles taught Mickey the game. Elvin threw right-handed and taught Mickey to bat left-handed against him. Charles threw left-handed, and when facing him, Mickey learned to bat from the right. Mantle set himself apart from the competition by being a natural switch-hitter. He would become the greatest switch-hitter in baseball history.

Mantle began playing semipro baseball in Baxter Springs, Kansas, at 15. When he was 17, a New York Yankees scout came to Baxter Springs to watch one of Mantle's older teammates. During the game, Mantle hit three home runs. While he was too young to sign to a professional contract at the time, the scout returned in 1949 after Mantle had graduated from high school and signed him.

Mantle's hitting ability was not in doubt, but he struggled defensively at shortstop. Before the 1951 season, Yankees manager Casey Stengel moved him to the outfield. Mantle was an established everyday player by August, and that fall he played in the first of 12 World Series. The Yankees won it all that year, but Mantle severely injured his knee after tripping over an exposed drainpipe while chasing a fly ball. While he recovered prior to the 1952 season, the injury robbed him of his blazing speed.

Mantle moved from right field to center field in 1952, taking over for the retired DiMaggio. That year he made the first of 18 consecutive All-Star teams. From 1953 to 1955 Mantle averaged 28 home runs, 98 RBI, and 118 runs scored per season. In 1955 he topped the AL with 37 home runs. In 1956 Mantle had his greatest season, winning the Triple Crown while batting .353 with 52 home runs and 130 RBI and winning the first of two consecutive AL MVPs. Mantle would win a third MVP Award in 1962 despite missing almost 40 games to yet another injury.

Mantle's last truly great year—and the last pennant for the Yankees' midcentury dynasty—came in 1964. From then on more injuries, and Mantle's noteworthy enjoyment of the New York nightlife, began to take their toll on him. Mantle retired prior to the 1969 season with 536 home runs, 1,676 runs scored, 1,509 RBI, 1,733 walks, and a .298 batting average. He had been named to 20 All-Star Games, won a Gold Glove for his play in center field in 1962, and was a part of seven Yankees teams that won the World Series, hitting a record 18 home runs in his 12 appearances in the Fall Classic. He was elected to the Hall of Fame in 1974.

AVG	OBP	SLG	OPS+	HR	RBI
.298	.421	.557	172	536	1,509

Position: **Outfield**
Batted: **Both**
Threw: **Right**
HT/WT: **5'11", 195 lb.**
Team: **New York Yankees (1951–68)**
Born: **10-20-1931**
Died: **8-13-1995**

Pedro Martínez

Like most boys in the Dominican Republic, Pedro Martínez and his brother Ramón grew up playing baseball, and both of them attracted the attention of pro scouts. Ramón signed with the Dodgers in 1984, and Pedro joined him in the Dodgers organization in 1988. Martínez made his big league debut in 1993, coming in to relieve his older brother in his first game.

Martínez posted a 10–5 record in 65 games while striking out 119 batters in 107 innings as a rookie. While those numbers suggested stardom, the Dodgers still traded him to the Montreal Expos. Once in Montreal, Martínez learned to command his 97 mph fastball, perfect his devastating changeup, and refine his already outstanding control to become one of the best pitchers in the game.

On June 3, 1995, Martínez retired the first 27 San Diego Padres batters he faced. If the game had not been tied at zero, it would have been only the 13th perfect game in baseball history. As it was, Martínez continued to pitch into the 10th inning, allowing a hit but earning a victory. Martínez took his game to new heights in 1997, going 17–8 with an NL-best 1.90 earned-run average while pitching 13 complete games and striking out 305 batters. He won his first Cy Young Award following the season, but was traded again, this time to the Boston Red Sox.

Martínez continued to shine in Boston. He went 19–7 in 1998. In 1999 he went 23–4 with a league-best 2.07 ERA and 313 strikeouts, winning the pitching Triple Crown and becoming the eighth pitcher to post two 300-strikeout

seasons. His 2000 season was even better. That year Martínez went 18–6 with a 1.74 ERA and 284 strikeouts. He allowed just 128 hits in 217 innings and set an all-time record for WHIP– walks plus hits divided by innings pitched–of 0.737. Making this even more astounding is that 1999 and 2000 were two of the most prolific offensive years in baseball history and Boston's Fenway Park was one of the most hitter-friendly ballparks in the game. No pitcher in the modern era has ever performed so much better than his peers. Not surprisingly, Martínez won the Cy Young Award in both seasons.

After battling shoulder problems in 2001, Martínez rebounded in 2002 with a 20–4 record, again leading the AL in ERA and strikeouts. Martínez once again led the league in WHIP, ERA, and winning percentage in 2003. In 2004 he helped the Red Sox win their first World Series title in 86 years.

Martínez signed with the Mets following the World Series and helped lead them to their first playoff appearance in six years in 2006. He ended his career with the Philadelphia Phillies and retired after the 2009 campaign.

Martínez ended his career with a record of 219–100, won five ERA titles en route to a career mark of 2.93, and captured six WHIP titles. When he retired, he was one of only four pitchers with at least 3,000 strikeouts and fewer than 1,000 walks, and he finished his career with an ERA+ of 154, which at the time stood as the highest mark ever for a starting pitcher in the modern era.

W	L	ERA	ERA+	IP	K	BB
219	100	2.93	154	2,827.1	3,154	760

Position: **Starting Pitcher**

Batted: **Right**

Threw: **Right**

HT/WT: **5'11", 170 lb.**

Teams: **Los Angeles Dodgers (1992–93), Montreal Expos (1994–97), Boston Red Sox (1998–2004), New York Mets (2005–8), Philadelphia Phillies (2009)**

Born: **10-25-1971**

Willie Mays

There are, probably, only four men who have a serious claim to being called the best baseball player in the history of the game: Babe Ruth, Oscar Charleston, Ty Cobb, and Willie Mays. Because he played in a fully integrated game against what most people would agree to be superior competition, many believe Mays has the strongest claim. He was certainly the best player in the game in the second half of the 20th century and is almost certainly the best ever all-around player, with tremendous home run power, incredible fielding ability, a high batting average, a great batter's eye, tremendous speed, and an extraordinary baseball IQ. Mays had virtually no weaknesses.

A multisport star from Westfield, Alabama, Mays signed with the Negro League Birmingham Black Barons in 1948 when he was in high school. He joined the New York Giants in 1950 and, following a brief time in the minors, was called up to New York and earned Rookie of the Year honors in 1951. His strong play down the stretch that year helped the Giants complete a historic comeback from a 13.5 game deficit to defeat the Brooklyn Dodgers for the National League pennant.

Mays spent most of the 1952 season and all of 1953 in the army but returned in 1954 to lead the league with a .345 batting average and 13 triples while blasting 41 homers and knocking in 110 runs. The Giants once again won the NL pennant and faced off that October in New York against the heavily favored Cleveland Indians.

With Game One tied 2–2 in the top of the eighth inning and runners on first and second, Indians batter Vic Wertz hit a long drive that would have been a home run in almost every ballpark except New York's Polo Grounds, which featured the deepest center field in all of baseball. Mays, playing a shallow center, took off running with his back to the ball and caught it over his shoulder some 460 feet from the plate. He then turned and fired the ball to the infield to keep the runners from advancing. The Giants went on to win the game and sweep the Series. Mays's play—known simply as "The Catch"—is widely considered to be the greatest defensive play in baseball history. It instantly made Willie Mays a legend.

For the next 20 seasons Mays was nothing short of excellent. He led the league in multiple home runs and in stolen bases each season for 1956–59. He was a six-time league leader in OPS+ and a five-time leader in slugging percentage. He was a two-time NL MVP (1954 and 1965). He was a 24-time All-Star and won 12 Gold Glove Awards in center field. He led the Giants to three pennants and that 1954 World Series title, and in his final season, he helped the New York Mets win the 1973 NL pennant.

Mays ranks among baseball's career leaders in virtually every offensive category and he is baseball's all-time leader in outfield putouts. He was elected to the Hall of Fame in 1979, but he was considered the greatest long before that happened. And he always will be.

AVG	OBP	SLG	OPS+	HR	RBI
.301	.384	.557	155	660	1,909

Position: **Outfield**
Batted: **Right**
Threw: **Right**
HT/WT: **5'10", 170 lb.**
Teams: **Birmingham Black Barons (1948), New York/San Francisco Giants (1951–72), New York Mets (1972–73)**
Born: **5-6-1931**

Joe Morgan

Joe Morgan was, according to most experts, the greatest all-around second baseman of all time. Like Mays, he was good at basically everything: He hit for average and power. He had a fantastic batting eye and would take more walks than most batters. He stole a lot of bases and was rarely caught stealing. He was a superb defensive second baseman and, according to most observers, one of the most intelligent men to ever play the game.

Growing up in Oakland, California, Morgan was known as "Little Joe" due to his being only 5'7" tall. He was a standout high school player but got no major league offers, likely because of his size. After one season of college baseball, however, he was signed by the Houston Colt .45s, which were later renamed the Houston Astros.

Early in his career, Morgan had trouble swinging quickly enough because he would keep his back elbow too low. His then-teammate, the future Hall of Famer Nellie Fox, suggested that Morgan flap his back arm, like a chicken, as a reminder to keep his elbow up. Morgan followed the advice and that flapping back elbow became a signature part of his game. More importantly, it quickened his swing and improved his hitting, leading to two All-Star game appearances while with Houston.

In late 1971 Morgan and two teammates were traded to the Cincinnati Reds. While many initially thought that the Astros got the better end of the deal due to the players they acquired in return, Morgan turned out to be the key to making a good Reds team into a great one.

Morgan led the league in runs, walks, and on-base percentage and made his third All-Star team in 1972. He improved even more in 1973 and won his first Gold Glove. After yet another All-Star appearance, Gold Glove, and even more offensive improvement in 1974, Morgan put together two of the greatest seasons ever for a second baseman in 1975 and 1976. He won the NL MVP Award in both years by hitting a combined .324/.456/.541 (177 OPS+) while averaging 22 home runs, 102 RBI, and 64 stolen bases and taking two more Gold Gloves. Most significantly, the Reds won the World Series in both 1975 and 1976. With Morgan recognized as the best player on those powerful Reds teams, his nickname transformed from "Little Joe" to "The Little General."

While 1975 and 1976 represented his peak performance, Morgan enjoyed a productive late career as well. He'd make three more All-Star teams and win one more Gold Glove with the Reds before returning to the Astros in 1980, during which he helped Houston reach the playoffs for the first time in franchise history. He put together two more strong seasons with the Giants in 1981 and 1982, and in 1983 he joined his old Reds teammates Pete Rose and Tony Pérez with the Phillies, helping lead them to the World Series. Following a final season with his hometown Oakland Athletics in 1984, Morgan retired, and then spent over two decades as one of the leading baseball TV broadcasters of his era.

Morgan was elected to the Hall of Fame in 1990. To this day he remains the standard against which all second basemen are measured.

AVG	OBP	SLG	OPS+	HR	RBI
.271	.392	.427	132	268	1,133

Position: **Second Base**
Batted: **Left**
Threw: **Right**
HT/WT: **5'7", 160 lb.**
Teams: **Houston Colt .45s/Astros (1963–71, 1980), Cincinnati Reds (1972–79), San Francisco Giants (1981–82), Philadelphia Phillies (1983), Oakland Athletics (1984)**
Born: **9-19-1943**
Died: **10-11-2020**

Stan Musial

Stan Musial was born to a mining family in Donora, Pennsylvania. His father wanted Stan to go to college and thus avoid the sort of hard labor he had endured, but Stan was far more taken with sports than studies. After initially refusing permission for his son to sign a minor league contract, the elder Musial relented and Stan began his career as a 17-year-old with the Cardinals' minor league affiliate, the Williamson Colts, of the Mountain State League in 1938.

Musial was originally a pitcher, but middling results, a shoulder injury, and good results in his limited batting appearances encouraged the Cardinals to make him a full-time outfielder in 1941. As a relatively self-taught hitter, Musial featured an unusual corkscrew-like hitting motion, beginning with his back nearly turned to the pitcher and uncoiling with an inside-out swing that gave him power to all fields. It worked extremely well for him, and he hit .379 with the Springfield Cardinals of the Western Association, leading that league with 26 home runs in just 87 games in 1941. After a quick promotion to the Rochester Red Wings later that summer, Musial arrived in St. Louis for a late season stint with the big league Cardinals in which he hit a blistering .426 in 12 games. He'd never play in the minors again.

In 1942, Musial hit .315 as the Cardinals' everyday left fielder, leading St. Louis to the NL pennant and a World Series title. The following year Musial truly came into his own, pacing the league in batting average, on-base percentage, slugging, OPS+, hits, doubles, triples, and total bases. He won the first of three NL MVP Awards that season and led the Cards back to the World Series, where they lost to the Yankees.

Musial and the Cardinals won the World Series again in 1944, and after missing the 1945 campaign due to service in the U.S. Navy, Musial returned in 1946, won his second MVP Award, and led St. Louis to its third World Series title in five seasons. His greatest offensive season was in 1948, when he led the league in virtually every significant offensive category, batting a career-high .376 but falling short of the Triple Crown by just one home run, and winning his third and final MVP.

While the Cardinals would never again reach the World Series in his career, Musial—now known as "Stan 'The Man' Musial"—continued as one of the game's premier hitters into the early '60s, winning four more batting titles. In 1962, at the age of 41, Musial made a run at the National League batting title, falling just 16 points short.

When Musial retired in 1963, he held the major league record for total bases and was the all-time leader in hits among National Leaguers. He also held the NL records for games played, plate appearances, at bats, runs, doubles, and runs batted in. He retired with a .331 average and 475 home runs, and he was the first player to accumulate both 400 homers and 3,000 hits in his career. In all, Musial won seven NL batting crowns.

Musial was elected to the Hall of Fame in 1969, drawing 93.2 percent of the vote.

AVG	OBP	SLG	OPS+	HR	RBI
.331	.417	.559	159	475	1,951

Position: **Outfield**
Batted: **Left**
Threw: **Left**
HT/WT: **6', 175 lb.**
Team: **St. Louis Cardinals (1941–63)**
Born: **11-21-1920**
Died: **1-19-2013**

Satchel Paige

Leroy Robert "Satchel" Paige was probably born in Mobile, Alabama, in 1906. No birth certificate was ever found, though, and Paige himself liked to be vague about his age, once famously saying, "Age is a question of mind over matter. If you don't mind, it doesn't matter." Such uncertainty is appropriate for Paige, however, in that his entire career was steeped in legend and tall tales, even if it was undeniably characterized by his out-standing pitching.

Paige began his professional career in 1926 and the lanky right-hander soon became the biggest drawing card in Black baseball due to his overpowering fastball. The official record of the teams for which Paige played in the 1920s and '30s is hard to determine due to his almost constant bouncing from team to team in search of larger paychecks and more interesting oppor-tunities. Throughout the 1930s, Paige likely pitched in hundreds of games a year between various leagues and countries even if the official statistics in baseball's record books only scratch the surface of his accomplishments.

Based on news reports and word of mouth, it is accepted that, in his prime, Paige possessed the fastest fastball since Walter Johnson. Later, when his heavy workloads began to give him arm trouble, Paige seamlessly switched from power pitcher to master of control. He was quite a show-man as well. On barnstorming tours, which often put Paige's teams up against somewhat inferior local competition, Paige would sometimes have his infielders sit down behind him and then strike out the side, demonstrating that he could defeat the opposition on his own.

Paige was over 40 by the time the National and American Leagues dropped their policy of racial segregation in 1947. The following year Cleveland Indians owner Bill Veeck signed him, and on July 9, 1948, he made his debut for a Cleveland club embroiled in one of the closest pennant races in history. Paige went 6–1 with three complete games and posted a 2.48 ERA down the stretch to help win the AL pennant in a one-game playoff against the Red Sox. Cleveland then captured the World Series title in six games against the Braves, with Paige becoming the first Black pitcher to appear in the World Series.

Paige pitched for Cleveland again in 1949 after which he spent three seasons with the St. Louis Browns, earning two All-Star Game selections. He returned to the minor leagues and barnstorming, continuing to pitch on and off throughout the 1950s and early '60s. He, amazingly, returned to the majors at the age of 59, to pitch a single game for the Kansas City Athletics. That day he tossed three innings of scoreless relief against the Red Sox, striking out a batter.

Paige remains the oldest person to ever play in a major league game. Not that he was done even then: on June 21, 1966, he appeared in a game for the Peninsula Grays of the Carolina League when he was only two weeks shy of 60–or so we think. No one was ever completely sure about anything when it came to Satchel Paige, apart from the fact that he was one of the greatest pitchers to ever play the game.

W	L	ERA	ERA+	IP	K	BB
124	82	2.73	150	1,751.2	1,501	463

Position: **Starting Pitcher**
Batted: **Right**
Threw: **Right**
HT/WT: **6'3", 180 lb.**
Teams: **Birmingham Black Barons
(1927–30), Cleveland Cubs (1931),
Pittsburgh Crawfords (1933–34, 1936),
Kansas City Monarchs (1941–47),
Memphis Red Sox (1943), Cleveland
Indians (1948–49), St. Louis Browns
(1951–53), Kansas City Athletics (1965)**
Born: **7-7-1906**
Died: **6-8-1982**

Frank Robinson

Frank Robinson grew up in Oakland, California, playing basketball alongside future NBA Hall of Famer Bill Russell and baseball alongside fellow future MLB star Curt Flood and his future major league teammate Vada Pinson. With that sort of talent all attending the same high school, it's no surprise that a lot of professional scouts came by, and in 1953, a scout for the Cincinnati Reds saw Robinson and signed him to a minor league contract.

Robinson broke into the majors as a 20-year-old in 1956 and achieved immediate stardom, tying a rookie record with 38 home runs and winning NL Rookie of the Year honors. Over the next two decades, Robinson gained a reputation for being one of the most feared hitters and base runners of all time while finding himself, year by year, at the top of the leaderboards alongside Mays, Aaron, and Mantle.

In 1961, Robinson won his first MVP Award, hitting .323 with 37 home runs and 124 RBI and leading the Reds to their first National League pennant in 21 years. He was even better in 1962, hitting .342 with 39 home runs, 136 RBI, and a major league–leading 134 runs scored. Robinson played his first 10 years with the Reds, hitting 30 home runs or more seven times and batting .300 five times.

Following the 1965 season, however, Reds owner and general manager Bill DeWitt Sr. felt that Robinson was due to decline, and traded him to the Baltimore Orioles for pitcher Milt Pappas. Robinson, already considered one of the game's most intense competitors, was determined to prove DeWitt wrong. And that he did, and then

some, leading many to consider the Robinson–Pappas trade one of the most lopsided deals in baseball history.

Robinson was baseball's best player in 1966, winning the Triple Crown while batting .316, hitting 49 home runs, and driving in 122 runs while leading the Orioles to their first World Series title and winning the World Series MVP Award. That November, Robinson became the first–and to date only–player to win MVP Awards in both leagues, and his 49 homers that year stood as the most hit by any American League player between 1962 and 1989. Robinson led the Orioles back to the World Series in 1969, 1970, and 1971.

Robinson was traded to the Dodgers before the 1972 season, and following one injury-plagued year there, he was traded to the Angels for whom he performed admirably in 1973 and 1974, making his final All-Star team as a player in the latter year. At the end of that season, he was traded to Cleveland, where he became the team's manager. That made Robinson the first Black person to manage an American or National League club. He continued to help Cleveland after he retired as a player following the 1976 season and would go on to manage several other teams.

In all, Robinson was a 14-time All-Star, batted .300 nine times, hit 30 home runs 11 times, and led his league in slugging four times and in runs scored three times. His 586 career home runs ranked fourth in major league history at the time of his retirement and currently stand at 10th.

He was elected to the Baseball Hall of Fame in his first year of eligibility, in 1982.

AVG	OBP	SLG	OPS+	HR	RBI
.294	.389	.537	154	586	1,812

Position: **Outfield**
Batted: **Right**
Threw: **Right**
HT/WT: **6'1", 183 lb.**
Teams: **Cincinnati Reds (1956–65),
Baltimore Orioles (1966–71), Los Angeles
Dodgers (1972), California Angels
(1973–74), Cleveland Indians (1974–76)**
Born: **8-31-1935**
Died: **2-7-2019**

Jackie Robinson

The impact Jackie Robinson had on Major League Baseball in becoming the first Black player in the 20th century to take the field in the American or National League, following nearly a century's worth of racial segregation, cannot be overstated. Robinson opened the door for countless others and will forever be remembered for his contribution to baseball and the world at large.

Raised in Pasadena, California, Robinson was an outstanding high school athlete, starring in baseball, football, basketball, and track. He went to UCLA on an athletic scholarship where he became the only person in the school's history to letter in four different sports. After leaving UCLA Robinson joined the army, where he was commissioned as a lieutenant, though he did not see combat during the war, in large part because of contrived court-martial proceedings against him stemming from an incident in which Robinson refused to give up his seat to a white person on an army transport bus. The army, unable to punish Robinson, discharged him instead.

Following his discharge, Robinson signed with the Kansas City Monarchs of the Negro Leagues for the 1945 season. He was soon scouted by Dodgers general manager Branch Rickey, who intended to sign top Black players to break baseball's color line. Rickey signed Robinson on October 23, 1945. Though Robinson was doubtless ready to compete in the big leagues, the Dodgers placed him with their top minor league team in Montreal, believing that a year of success in the minors might make it easier for white audiences to accept a Black player in the majors.

Robinson made his major league debut on April 15, 1947. While he was cheered at home and in cities with large Black fan bases, Robinson nonetheless was taunted by opposing crowds and experienced rough physical play by opponents. Rickey had picked Robinson to integrate baseball not only because of his superior baseball skills, but also because of his intelligence and temperament. Robinson faced the abuse with honor and grace and quickly earned the respect of his teammates, fans, and even many of his opponents. He also quickly established himself as one of the finest players in the game.

In 1947 Robinson led the league in stolen bases, won the Rookie of the Year Award, and received some MVP votes while helping the Dodgers to a National League pennant. He was named the NL MVP in 1949 while leading the league in hitting with a .342 average and 37 steals as well as knocking in a career-high 124 runs. In his 10 seasons with the Dodgers, Robinson hit .313/.410/.477 (133 OPS+) while scoring 972 runs, notching 1,563 hits, stealing 200 bases, and making the All-Star team six times. The Dodgers won six pennants in Robinson's tenure and captured the franchise's first World Series title in 1955.

Following his retirement, Robinson served on the board of directors of the National Association for the Advancement of Colored People and remained active in civil rights and politics until late in his life. He was elected to the Hall of Fame in his first year of eligibility in 1962. He was the first Black player inducted.

Every April 15, Jackie Robinson Day commemorates the day Robinson made his major league debut. On that day, all players, coaches, managers, and umpires wear Robinson's uniform number of 42.

Position: **Second Base**
Batted: **Right**
Threw: **Right**
HT/WT: **5'11", 195 lb.**
Teams: **Kansas City Monarchs
(1945), Brooklyn Dodgers (1947–56)**
Born: **1-31-1919**
Died: **10-24-1972**

AVG	OBP	SLG	OPS+	HR	RBI
.313	.410	.477	133	141	761

Álex Rodríguez

Born in New York to Dominican parents, Álex Rodríguez–known by his nickname "A-Rod"– spent most of his childhood in Miami, where he was a star high school player. By the summer of 1993 he was considered the top amateur baseball player in the country, and was consequently chosen by the Seattle Mariners as the top overall pick in the draft.

Rodríguez rocketed through the Mariners system, going from Single-A to the majors in the space of just three months. He'd shuttle back and forth between Seattle and Triple-A until early 1996 when he broke out as one of baseball's top stars, leading the league in hitting with a .358 average while hitting 36 homers and 123 RBI. He would not have anything less than a great season for the next 15 years.

Rodríguez's first of eight 40+-homer seasons came in 1998 in which he hit 42 round trippers and led the American League with 213 hits. Over the next two years he'd hit 42 and 41 more homers, respectively. In late 2000 A-Rod became a free agent and signed a $252 million contract with the Texas Rangers, making him baseball's highest-paid player. Many questioned whether *any* baseball player was worth that kind of money, but A-Rod more than earned his pay, leading the league in home runs in all three years he played in Texas, with 52 in 2001, 57 in 2002, and 47 in 2003 while winning his first MVP Award.

Rodríguez was traded to the Yankees before the 2004 season. Although he had only played shortstop in his career to that point, he deferred to Yankees captain Derek Jeter and accepted a move to third base, where he'd play for the remainder of his career. In 2005 A-Rod broke the Yankees' single-season record for home runs by a right-handed hitter with 48 and earned his second MVP Award. He raised that record to 54 two years later, once again taking home MVP hardware. In 2009 he put to rest criticisms about hitting poorly in the playoffs when he dominated the Twins in the American League Division Series and the Los Angeles Angels in the AL Championship Series. He was likewise a strong contributor in the Yankees' World Series victory over the Philadelphia Phillies.

A-Rod's final years as a player were characterized by periodic greatness but considerable controversy. On August 4, 2010, he hit his 600th career home run, but by 2012 he'd be embroiled in a performance-enhancing drug scandal and would be suspended for the entire 2014 season. Never a popular player during his career due to the perception that he was arrogant, A-Rod became particularly loathed at this time. He returned in 2015 as a notably humbler person, however. He played quite well, too, which went a long way toward rehabilitating his reputation.

A-Rod retired following the 2016 season with a career .295 batting average and 696 home runs, which ranks fifth on the all-time list. He is also a member of the 3,000-hit club and is one of only five players to finish his career with over 2,000 runs batted in. He was a 14-time All-Star, won three MVP Awards, 10 Silver Slugger Awards, two Gold Glove Awards and stands as the career record holder for grand slams with 25.

AVG	OBP	SLG	OPS+	HR	RBI
.295	.380	.550	140	696	2,086

Positions: **Shortstop, Third Base**
Batted: **Right**
Threw: **Right**
HT/WT: **6'3", 230 lb.**
Teams: **Seattle Mariners (1994–2000), Texas Rangers (2001–3), New York Yankees (2004–16)**
Born: **7-27-1975**

Babe Ruth

There is no more famous player in all of baseball history than Babe Ruth. He began as one of the game's greatest pitchers, but Ruth truly revolutionized the game when he devoted himself to hitting full-time, turning what was to that point a game of base hits, fast runners, and low scores into one where the home run became the signature accomplishment.

Born in Baltimore to a saloonkeeper, young George Herman Ruth Jr.—nicknamed "Babe"—was sent to St. Mary's Industrial School for Boys, a reformatory school and orphanage, at age seven due to his constant behavioral problems. It was there where he learned the game of baseball from Brother Matthias Boutlier, the school's disciplinarian and a skilled ballplayer in his own right.

Ruth achieved renown as a teenage baseball player, and after turning 19 he signed with the then-minor-league Baltimore Orioles. Ruth excelled for the Orioles, but team owner Jack Dunn experienced financial problems that summer and was forced to sell the contracts of his best players, Ruth included, to other teams. The Red Sox offered the highest price for Ruth, and so he headed to Boston.

Ruth began his major league career as a pitcher, breaking out as a major star in 1916 when he won 23 games with a league-best 1.75 ERA while pitching nine shutouts. Ruth's pitching was a big reason the Red Sox won the World Series that year and in 1918 as well. By 1919 the Red Sox realized that Ruth's hitting abilities were stronger than his pitching skills, and he began to pitch less and less. While still technically a two-way player that year, Ruth set a new home run record with 29. And that's when things really began to get interesting.

Because of his high salary—and because his love of nightlife made people nervous about his career—the Red Sox sold Ruth's contract to the Yankees before the 1920 season. Once in New York, Ruth's career ascended to even greater heights and his home run totals reached epic proportions. Ruth would not hit fewer than 40 home runs in 10 of his next 12 seasons, with a then-unthinkable 54 home runs in 1920, 59 in 1921, 60 in 1927, and 54 in 1928. He was no one-dimensional player, either, as he led the league in on-base percentage, slugging percentage, walks, total bases, and runs scored nearly every season through the 1920s. Along the way he led the Yankees to seven American League pennants and four World Series wins, launching a Yankees dynasty which would last for over 40 years. In 1923 the Yankees opened their new ballpark, Yankee Stadium, which carried the nickname "The House That Ruth Built." By the time he retired in 1935, Ruth had hit 714 home runs, which stood as the major league record before Hank Aaron broke it in 1974. Ruth is still third on the all-time home run list.

Babe Ruth's historical importance cannot be overstated. His ascendance transformed what has since come to be known as the Deadball Era, when pitching dominated, into the modern era. His nickname—"The Sultan of Swat"—stands as testament to his slugging prowess. As is the fact that his last name has turned into a synonym for accomplishments of heroic proportions: "Ruthian."

AVG	OBP	SLG	OPS+	HR	RBI
.342	.474	.690	206	714	2,214

Positions: **Outfield, Pitcher**
Batted: **Left**
Threw: **Left**
HT/WT: **6'2", 215 lb.**
Teams: **Boston Red Sox (1914–19),**
New York Yankees (1920–34),
Boston Braves (1935)
Born: **2-6-1895**
Died: **8-16-1948**

Mike Schmidt

Possessing an outstanding glove, tremendous power, and a keen batter's eye, Mike Schmidt is considered the greatest all-around third baseman in major league history.

Schmidt was a star high school and college player in Ohio. He earned All-American honors in 1970 and led the Ohio University Bobcats to the College World Series that year. His amateur exploits made him worthy of a second-round pick by the Philadelphia Phillies in 1971.

Because the Phillies were such a bad team in the early 1970s, Schmidt was able to crack the starting lineup, despite spending little time in the minors. Initially overmatched at the plate, Schmidt's copious strikeouts—though more than offset by his power and the walks he drew—made him unpopular with Phillies fans. But Schmidt turned things around by 1974, when he hit .282 and smacked 36 homers, which led the National League. It was first of three consecutive home run championships for Schmidt and eight NL home run crowns in all.

Schmidt averaged 36 homers, 102 RBI, over 100 walks a year, and an OPS+ of 147 between 1974 and 1979, while earning four All-Star appearances and four Gold Gloves. He raised his game in 1980, to lead the league with 48 homers, 121 RBI, a slugging percentage of .624, an OPS of 1.004, and an OPS+ of 171 while taking home yet another Gold Glove, making another All-Star appearance, and winning his first MVP Award. More importantly for Phillies fans—who had come to believe that Schmidt and the Phillies would never be truly great—he led the Phillies to a six-game World Series victory that season, taking home World Series MVP honors to boot.

Schmidt won his second straight MVP trophy in 1981 while heading the National League in nearly every significant offensive category. Schmidt also won the 1981 All-Star Game with a dramatic late inning home run. He was once again dominant in the 1983 season, leading the league in home runs and walks while helping the Phillies to another NL pennant. Another home run and RBI title—and the now-expected All-Star Game and Gold Glove selections—followed in 1984. Schmidt won a third MVP in 1986, leading the league in HRs for the eighth and final time and in RBI for the fourth and final time.

A shoulder injury led to a decline at the plate for Schmidt during the 1988 season. Dissatisfied with anything less than his usual greatness, Schmidt retired, somewhat unexpectedly, on May 29, 1989. That season he became the first retired player to be voted onto the All-Star team, and while he did not play, he did appear at the game. Schmidt finished his career with 548 career home runs, 509 of which came while playing third base, which remains an all-time record at the position. He likewise holds the record for RBI as a third baseman with 1,419 of his 1,595 runs batted in coming while playing the hot corner. Schmidt is also one of only three players, along with Willie Mays and Ken Griffey Jr., to take 10 Gold Gloves and hit at least 500 home runs. He is the only infielder ever to do so.

Schmidt was elected to the Hall of Fame in 1995 with what was, at the time, the fourth-highest voting percentage ever, 96.52 percent.

Position: **Third Base**
Batted: **Right**
Threw: **Right**
HT/WT: **6'2", 195 lb.**
Team: **Philadelphia Phillies (1972–89)**
Born: **9-27-1949**

AVG	OBP	SLG	OPS+	HR	RBI
.267	.380	.527	148	548	1,595

Tris Speaker

Tristram Edgar Speaker–known as "Tris"–was born in Hubbard, Texas, where he rode horses and worked as a ranch hand. Tris broke his arm after falling from a horse, which forced him to become a left-handed player, giving him an advantage as a hitter.

Speaker played minor league ball in Texas before his contract was sold to the Boston Americans–soon to be renamed the Red Sox–toward the end of the 1907 season. After a brief stint with the Little Rock Travelers of the Southern League, Speaker was reacquired by Boston later that year. As 1909 dawned, Speaker was Boston's everyday center fielder. He would start in center for every team for which he played for the next 20 seasons while establishing himself as one of the greatest defensive center fielders the game has ever seen. Speaker was known for playing a very shallow center field, which helped him lead AL center fielders in assists eight times, while his speed and his ability to run down balls hit over his head helped him lead AL center fielders in putouts seven times. His 450 career assists still rank first in big league history among center fielders, and his 6,783 putouts rank second among center fielders.

Of course, defense was only part of his game. A tremendous contact hitter who could drive the ball into the gaps and down the line, Speaker led the league in doubles eight times in his career, which was the mark of a batter's power in the days before home runs exploded in the 1920s. Speaker first paced the circuit in doubles in 1912, when he hit 53 two-baggers, while also leading the league in home runs with 10 and on-base

percentage at a .464 clip. He also became one of only two players to ever hit 50 doubles and steal 50 bases in the same season. When the Red Sox won their second of nine World Series titles in 1912, Speaker was undeniably the club's top star.

Speaker guided the Red Sox to another World Series title in 1915, but Boston, balking at Speaker's demands for a pay raise and believing his best years were behind him, traded him to Cleveland. That was a mistake as, in Speaker's first season with the Indians, he led the AL in hits (211), doubles (51), batting average (.386), on-base percentage (.470), and slugging percentage (.502).

Speaker took over as Cleveland's player-manager during the 1919 season. In 1920, he led the team to their first World Series championship. Within a few years Speaker would be the first manager to make a point to platoon players in his lineup, matching up right-handed hitters against lefties and lefty hitters against righties. Unlike a lot of player-managers of his era, Speaker remained a productive everyday player as well, posting career bests in average (.389) and on-base percentage (a league-leading .479) in 1925 at age 37.

Speaker rounded out his career with single seasons in Washington and Philadelphia, where he teamed up with his longtime competitor Cobb in 1928. Speaker retired after that season at age 40. When he did so, he was the all-time leader in doubles with 792 and continues to hold the record to this day.

AVG	OBP	SLG	OPS+	HR	RBI
.345	.428	.500	158	117	1,531

Position: **Outfield**
Batted: **Left**
Threw: **Left**
HT/WT: **5'11", 193 lb.**
Teams: **Boston Red Sox (1907–15),
Cleveland Indians (1916–26),
Washington Senators (1927),
Philadelphia Athletics (1928)**
Born: **4-4-1888**
Died: **12-8-1958**

Honus Wagner

Hall of Fame manager John McGraw called Honus Wagner "the nearest thing to a perfect player." And he was, indeed, the total package. Wagner hit for average and for power. He was a superior base runner. While he was primarily a shortstop—and a fantastic one at that—he played every position on the diamond at some point in his major league career except for catcher.

Nicknamed "The Flying Dutchman" due to his superb speed and German heritage, Johannes Peter "Honus" Wagner was born to immigrant parents in Carnegie, Pennsylvania, and dropped out of school at 12 to work with his father in the coal mines. In their free time he and his brothers played sandlot baseball. When older brother Albert was signed to a professional contract, he told his manager to take a look at the younger Honus as he was an even better player.

Wagner was signed to a professional contract and played for five teams in three different leagues in 1895. The following year, Wagner played for Ed Barrow—who would become the architect of the New York Yankees dynasties of the 1920s and '30s—of the Paterson, New Jersey, Silk Sox. He performed so well there that Barrow realized Wagner was too good for the minors and sold his contract to the Louisville Colonels of the National League. Between 1897 and 1899 Wagner hit .322 while showcasing outstanding defense in 361 games for Louisville. When the team was dissolved by the National League after the 1899 campaign, Wagner joined the Pittsburgh Pirates.

Wagner broke out as a superstar in his first season in Pittsburgh, leading the league in batting (.381), doubles (45), triples (22), slugging (.573), OPS (1.007), and OPS+ (176). Wagner hit .300 or better for 15 straight seasons, winning eight National League batting titles, leading the NL in doubles seven times, triples three times, stolen bases five times, RBI four times, slugging percentage six times, and on-base percentage four times. Throughout this period Wagner was also known as one of the game's nimblest defenders and fastest runners, despite his stocky build, muscular frame, and bowed legs. Wagner's Pirates won the NL pennant in 1903. That year's World Series was the first one ever played, and Wagner had the distinction of collecting the first-ever RBI and first-ever stolen base in World Series history. The Pirates won the World Series in 1909.

When Wagner retired following the 1917 season, he had totaled 3,420 hits, 643 doubles, 1,739 runs, 1,732 RBI, and 723 stolen bases to go with a .328 batting average. While they have since been surpassed by other players, most of those marks were National League records at the time.

Wagner also happens to appear on the most valuable baseball card of all time. The card, produced by the American Tobacco Company in 1909, is exceedingly rare as Wagner refused to allow mass production of it either because he did not want children to buy the tobacco products with which the cards came or because he wanted more compensation for his likeness. Either way, only a few dozen were printed, and those which have survived have sold at auction for millions of dollars.

Wagner entered the Hall of Fame in its first induction class in 1936.

AVG	OBP	SLG	OPS+	HR	RBI
.328	.391	.467	151	101	1,732

Position: **Shortstop**
Batted: **Right**
Threw: **Right**
HT/WT: **5'11", 200 lb.**
Teams: **Louisville Colonels (1897–99), Pittsburgh Pirates (1900–17)**
Born: **2-24-1874**
Died: **12-6-1955**

Ted Williams once said, "All I want out of life is that when I walk down the street folks will say, 'There goes the greatest hitter that ever lived.'" Williams can certainly lay claim to that title, with most experts considering him to be neck and neck with Babe Ruth as the greatest hitter of them all.

Learning to play the game on the sandlots of San Diego, Williams played 42 games for the minor league San Diego Padres of the Pacific Coast League in 1936 before he even graduated high school. The following year he returned to the Padres and, at only 18, hit .291 with 23 homers and 96 RBI in 138 games. That turned the heads of the Boston Red Sox, who signed him and sent him to the Minneapolis Millers for the 1938 campaign. Williams won the American Association Triple Crown that year with a .366 average, 43 home runs, and 142 RBI, dramatically outpacing his competition.

Williams enjoyed his greatest season in 1941. Williams was batting .39955 as the campaign entered its final day. That would have rounded up to .400, and his manager offered to bench Williams in order to ensure he hit the mark. Williams declined, however, wanting to earn his .400 on the field, not the bench. He played that day and torched Philadelphia A's pitchers for six hits in eight at bats to finish the season at .406. No hitter has hit .400 in the more than 80 years since.

Williams won the Triple Crown in 1942 with a .356 average, 36 home runs, and 137 RBI and seemed poised to continue to dominate the batting leaderboards for years on end, but history had something else in mind. With the outbreak of World War II, Williams joined the Naval Reserve and went on active duty as a second lieutenant and naval aviator. His time in the service caused him to miss the 1943, 1944, and 1945 seasons. Williams returned at the top of his game in 1946, winning the MVP and leading Boston to its only AL pennant in his 19 seasons with the club.

Williams won yet another Triple Crown in 1947 and another batting title in 1948, and he led the AL in home runs and tied for the league lead in RBI in 1949 while winning the MVP Award. He experienced a slight falloff in 1950 and 1951 due to an elbow injury, but they were only poor seasons by Williams's lofty standards. Williams was called for active duty with the Marines in 1952, serving as a fighter pilot in Korea. Williams never regretted his service, but his time away for both World War II and Korea cost him an estimated 800 hits, over 150 home runs, and nearly 600 RBI over the course of his career. Not that his career numbers were lacking. When Williams retired following the 1960 season–hitting a home run in his final at bat–he finished with a lifetime .344 batting average, a major league record .482 on-base percentage, 521 home runs, 2,021 walks, and 1,839 RBI.

Williams was elected to the Hall of Fame in 1966. He used his induction speech to campaign for the recognition of former Negro League players by the Hall of Fame. Five years later the Hall inducted its first former Negro Leaguers, with fellow legends Oscar Charleston, Josh Gibson, and Satchel Paige eventually joining Williams in Cooperstown.

AVG	OBP	SLG	OPS+	HR	RBI
.344	.482	.634	191	521	1,839

Position: **Outfield**
Batted: **Left**
Threw: **Right**
HT/WT: **6'3", 205 lb.**
Team: **Boston Red Sox (1939–60)**
Born: **8-30-1918**
Died: **7-5-2002**

Statistics Glossary

Each player in this book has a grid of some key statistics. One set is for hitters, and another is for pitchers. Here is a brief explanation of what those statistics represent.

For Hitters

Batting average (BA): A player's hits divided by the total times at bat. .300 and above are considered to be high batting averages.

On-base percentage (OBP): How often a batter has been on base, calculated by adding together a batter's hits, walks, and the number of times he's been hit by pitches, then dividing that number by his at bats plus walks plus the times he's been hit by pitches plus his sacrifice flies. It's more advanced than batting average. Over .350 is excellent. Over .400 is absolutely outstanding.

Slugging percentage (SLG): A measure of effectiveness of a player's offensive efforts, calculated by taking the total number of bases a player gets to divided by his at bats. SLG measures how powerful a hitter is, keeping in mind that home runs are worth more than triples, which are worth more than doubles, which are worth more than singles.

OPS+: A measure of a player's total offensive contribution, achieved by adding on-base percentage and slugging percentage together and then adjusting that number in a way that compares the player to other hitters in the league. An OPS+ of 100 is league average. So anything above 100 is above average, and anything below 100 is below average. A score of 150 is 50 percent better than the league average; a score of 85 is 15 percent below league average; and so on.

Home runs (HR): A four-base hit, usually accomplished by hitting the ball over the fence or into the stands. There are a lot of nicknames for home runs, including homer, dinger, tater, round tripper, bomb, and blast.

Runs batted in (RBI): An RBI is awarded to a batter whenever a runner on base or the batter scores as a result of a batter's plate appearance, usually by a hit, a walk, or a sacrifice fly. 100 or more RBI in a season is outstanding.

For Pitchers

Wins (W): A player receives a win when he is the pitcher at the time his team takes the lead for good in a game. For many years winning 20 games in a season or 300 in a career was considered outstanding. Because of various changes in the game regarding how pitchers are used, these days 15 wins or more in a season or 200 wins in a career is considered a more reasonable standard of excellence.